Empowering the
Self-Directed Team

D1531899

Written by Patricia Wilson
Edited by National Press Publications

NATIONAL PRESS PUBLICATIONS
A Division of Rockhurst College Continuing Education Center, Inc.
6901 West 63rd Street • P.O. Box 2949
Shawnee Mission, Kansas 66201-1349
1-800-258-7248 • 1-913-432-7757

National Seminars endorses nonsexist language.
However, to make this handbook clear, consistent
and easy to read, we've used the generic "he"
throughout when referring to both males and females.
The copy is not intended to be sexist.

Empowering the Self-Directed Team

Printed in the United States of America.

3 4 5 6 7 8 9 10

ISBN 1-55852-125-9

Empowering the Self-Directed Team

Table of Contents

Introduction

WHY SELF-DIRECTED TEAMS?

Can you remember when business roles were pretty clear? The boss gave the orders, chose the people to carry out these orders and stayed on their backs until the work was done. The employees followed the orders, collected their paychecks and kept their thoughts and ideas to themselves. The organizational hierarchy ensured that everyone knew his job expectations, his reporting status and the extent of his authority. This hierarchy was depicted as a pyramid, with the boss at the top and everyone else in descending order down to the line workers at the broad base.

Your place on the pyramid determined your job in a straightforward way. You knew exactly how you fit into the organization, what job you were expected to do, whom you did it for and whom you could pass it on to. You also knew which route to take to reach the upper levels of the pyramid.

That picture is changing! Today organizations must deal with a hierarchy that blurs the lines of authority. You may find yourself reporting to more than one person, having many job responsibilities and working in several different areas. At the same time, you may have more responsibility, more personal power and more input on how the job is done.

Organizations often deal with this change in hierarchy by creating working groups, quality circles, management teams or departmental committees. These "self-directed" teams are used as a basic organizational building block. People are recruited for their teamwork potential, freed from traditional bureaucracy and paid for their performance. The idea is not new. Many believe that it is of Japanese origin, but in fact, teamwork has been the bedrock of Western military thinking for hundreds of years.

Why do these teams work? Because people in groups of 10 to 30 can get to know each other well, learn to depend on each other for support and move swiftly ahead without the burden of bureaucracy. Why do some of these teams fail? There are three main reasons:

- Because upper and middle management misunderstand the concept of the self-managing team.

- Because some members see the team as an opportunity to "empire build."

- Because team members, supervisor-leaders and managers are poorly trained.

Let's assume that your organization has decided to institute self-managing teams. Employees are brought together so that they can work as a team on common issues and achieve common goals. A team leader appointed from within the group motivates the team members to work on these issues and goals.

- What happens when you are appointed team leader?

- How do you empower yourself to be a team leader?

- How do you empower your fellow team members?

- How do you avoid the pitfalls that lead to failure of the team?

- How do you develop a framework for your team?

- How do you meet the needs of the team members?

The answers to these questions are important to your success as a team leader and ultimately to your career goals. There's no one to talk to — you're the first team leader in your organization. There are no books in the company library — the idea is too new. Your boss seems to expect you to know all the answers — no doubt through some kind of mental osmosis! It feels as if you're in a Catch-22 situation.

That is why this handbook was written. It will give you the answers to these questions and to the many other questions you may have by offering practical suggestions and guidelines. More importantly, you will discover that leading a self-directed team means that you also must become a self-empowered leader. The personal self-empowerment process is an integral part of this handbook and works in tandem with team self-empowerment. By empowering yourself, you can empower others.

1

WHAT IS EMPOWERMENT?

Until the moment you are chosen as leader for your team, the hierarchical changes within your organization probably do not affect you directly. But as a team leader you are responsible for bringing a group of people together, creating a common vision and, most importantly, convincing, persuading, motivating, even coercing them to peak performance.

These team members are people you work with every day: people who are more experienced, less experienced, older, younger, of the same sex, of the opposite sex, friend or foe. Their enthusiasms range from burned-out to turned-on or just plain disinterested.

You have no real authority over your team members. You can't tell them what to do, and you can't simply sell them on the idea of being a team. Somehow you must find a way to light a fire within them that will continue to fuel itself.

Faced with this challenge, you do the one thing you are sure that a team leader should do: You call a meeting.

It's 9:10 a.m. The meeting was scheduled to start at 9 a.m. So far, you're the only one in the room. Several frantic phone calls finally round up your reluctant team. By 9:30 a.m., the last straggler is in place.

You're feeling more than a little uncomfortable as you realize that everybody is waiting for you to say something. Hesitantly, you begin to explain the boss' expectations for the team. Out of the corner of your eye, you catch someone's yawn. Only one person is listening intently to you: The person who also happens to be your best friend in the office.

At the end of your explanations, you ask if anyone has any questions. No one does. If anyone would care to comment. No one would. If anyone has any ideas. No one does.

You remind everyone that the team will meet each week at the same time to check back on its activities. Finally, you thank everybody for coming and signal the end of the meeting. No one thanks you for your leadership. It is 9:45 a.m.

As your team members file out, you realize that it is going to be even harder than you thought to bring this group to peak performance. With a sinking feeling, you remember that your boss has made it pretty clear that your next performance appraisal will be based on how well you handle your assignment as team leader. You know that this is a wonderful opportunity to put your career on the fast track, but you already suspect that you're doomed for the slow lane.

How do you get your team turned on? How do you light that internal fire? How do you empower team members to become peak performers?

WHAT IS EMPOWERMENT?

To "empower" means to enable, allow or permit. It can be either self-initiated or initiated by others. There are two aspects to organizational empowerment:

1. Building, developing and increasing power through cooperation, sharing and working together

2. Making a commitment to common goals, taking risks and demonstrating initiative and creativity

Empowerment encourages employees to participate actively in the decision-making process. It allows them to achieve recognition, involvement and a sense of worth in their jobs, thus improving job satisfaction and morale.

How on earth are you supposed to do all that with your team? In fact, how do you empower yourself to empower others?

SELF-EMPOWERMENT

Imagine that you always have wanted to build your own house. To accomplish this, you could do a number of things to learn about building a house. You could attend seminars on house building; you could watch carpenters at work on a house; you could take lessons in power-tool use. Once you have gathered all the information you need to build a house, you acquire land, draw up the blue prints, order lumber and purchase tools. At this moment, you have the power to build the house because you possess the knowledge, the materials and the tools that you need. But, the house won't be built until you empower yourself to start building.

In the same way, you must empower yourself to be a team leader before you can empower your team. Being an empowered team leader means participating, not just leading. It means accepting ideas and opinions other than your own. It means listening and providing positive feedback.

If you are like most, you sometimes think you never will reach that level of leadership. In fact, you sometimes may wonder why you don't act this way when you know it's effective.

The reason is that your actions often are determined by your core beliefs about yourself. Your first step in empowering yourself, and then your team, is to discover your own core beliefs. In the next chapter, we'll discuss your core beliefs and how they affect your leadership.

2

HOW CORE BELIEFS CAN HINDER EMPOWERMENT

WHAT ARE CORE BELIEFS?

The ideas that you hold about yourself and the world around you make up your core beliefs. Usually these beliefs are unconscious and unexamined, but almost every action you take is influenced by them. They are often the root cause of why you act the way you do.

WHERE DO THESE BELIEFS COME FROM?

Many core beliefs come from your past, particularly from the adults you knew in your childhood. In fact, most of your core beliefs were formed before you were six years old. If adults told you that you were bright, lovable and creative, you enjoyed a positive belief in your abilities. On the other hand, if adults belief in your abilities. On the other hand, if adults said you were stupid, lazy or useless, their negative statements created a core belief in your own unworthiness. These are very simplistic, black-and-white statements of belief. Usually a core belief is a little more complicated. It's based on conflicting statements from the adults around you, your own experiences when dealing with the belief and your expectations of yourself and your behavior.

If your core beliefs can be seen as explaining why you behave in certain ways, then they also play a part in your behavior as a team leader. It's important, therefore, to examine any beliefs that may affect this particular aspect of your life.

HOW DO YOU DETERMINE WHICH ARE CORE BELIEFS?

A core belief is so basic that you never stop to think about it. You just presume that "this is who I am, how I behave, and there's nothing I can do about it."

There are five basic categories of core beliefs:

1. Self-responsibility

2. Self-worth

3. Positive outlook

4. Personal security

5. Attitude toward change

CORE BELIEF ONE: SELF-RESPONSIBILITY

Let's examine your beliefs about responsibility. To do so, answer the following questions.

1. When something doesn't work out the way you expected it to, what do you say to yourself?

2. When a misfortune occurs in your life, how do you react?

3. When someone does something to you that you don't like, what do you think to yourself?

4. What are the "have to's" in your life?

5. Are your choices in life limited or unlimited?

Do your answers sound like some of the following?

- "Why does this always have to happen to me?"
- "It's all his (her) fault."
- "Why can't I be lucky like other people?"
- "I'm always the one who gets the raw end of the deal."
- "I always have to do what is expected of me. I have no choice."
- "I wish I had freedom to make some decisions for myself."
- "I wish my life could be different."

Answers such as these reflect a core belief that you have no power over your own life. In fact, your core belief is that you cannot be responsible for your life. People with this core belief share certain characteristics.

- They feel victimized by a life circumstance.
- Events often immobilize their actions.
- They attempt to place blame on something or someone else.
- They see themselves as victims.
- They feel helpless and out of control.

Perhaps this is how you felt when the boss appointed you as team leader. Part of you was excited at the prospect, but the core belief inside may have whispered, "Why me? I can't do this. I don't know how. My boss is just trying to put me in a position where I can't succeed. The team members won't help me either. They have no reason to want me to succeed. I'm doomed to fail at this."

The self-responsibility core belief underlies everything that you try to do. How can you change this core belief from one of helplessness to one of self-responsibility?

1. Accept what happens. Don't deny the anxiety, the frustration or even the stress, but at the same time, allow yourself to feel some anticipation, excitement and confidence.

2. Change your reactions to the event. It is not so much what happens to you that matters, but how you react to it.

3. Consider every event in your life as a learning experience that can empower you to move on in your life.

4. Take responsibility. Decide how you want to deal with this event. List positive alternatives, seek out people who have the experience or information you can use, model successful people and increase your own knowledge and skill.

CORE BELIEF TWO: SELF-WORTH

Someone once defined self-worth as "loving yourself as you are, warts and all!" To not only accept yourself, but to love yourself as an imperfect, changing, growing, worthwhile person is the essence of self-worth.

How do you feel about yourself? You may be surprised at your answers to the following questions.

1. Do you feel that you are a lovable person?

2. Do you feel confident in your abilities:

    • in personal relationships?
    • in social settings?
    • in business dealings?

3. Do you often wish that you were like someone else that you admire? Why?

4. Do you find it easy to accept praise and compliments from other people?

5. Do you feel that you deserve success in your life?

If your feelings of self-worth are low, you may experience doubts about your ability to handle the job of team leader. You may even believe that you don't deserve this responsibility because you are not "good enough." Such doubts will transfer to your interactions with the team. If you don't believe in yourself and your abilities, neither will your team. A proverb says, "If you love yourself, then you can give love away." If you believe in yourself, you give this belief to others.

Perhaps you feel that your self-worth could use a little boosting. Try some of these suggestions.

1. Take stock of yourself. Make a list of everything that you know you can do. The list will include your abilities, skills, talents, strengths, experience and knowledge. List everything, from your ability to handle a dozen different jobs at once to the time you dealt with that angry client. Don't worry about being egotistical. You simply are taking pride in your accomplishments.

2. When you attend meetings, sit erectly. You will give the team the subliminal message that you are in control. Resist the temptation to look down at your notes. Instead, maintain eye contact as you speak to the team.

3. When you talk to the team, use positive, affirming language. Focus on what is going right, rather than on what is going wrong. Compliment your members as often as you can — even arriving on time deserves praise!

4. Similarly, when you talk about yourself and your ideas, use the same positive, affirming language. Watch out for self-defeating phrases such as, "Well, this is probably a silly idea, but I thought we could..."; "I'm not really an expert, but..."; or "You probably won't agree with me, but I thought..."

5. Allow input from your team members. Listen to their ideas with an open mind. People with low self-worth often will try to disguise it by putting down other people and their ideas. Being open to your team members affirms your belief in your own self-worth.

6. Finally, accept the successes that come to you. Although we are not all born with the same abilities and qualities, we are all born with the same right to achieve success in our own ways. Being appointed a team leader is a success that you deserve.

CORE BELIEF THREE: POSITIVE OUTLOOK

When you see a glass containing half the water it can hold, do you perceive it as half empty or half full? Do you see life as a problem to be overcome or as an opportunity to be experienced? Your mental outlook on all the events of your life will influence its outcome greatly. In many ways, you are a self-fulfilling prophecy: You get what you expect.

What do you expect from life? The following questions will help you determine whether your glass is half empty or half full.

1. When people around you are sick, do you expect to be the next one to catch the office cold, flu, etc.?

2. Do you automatically list the negatives to a difficult situation before you look at the positive aspects?

3. Do you generally expect the worst to happen?

4. Do you find yourself thinking:

   "Life is hard. It's all a struggle."
   "Nothing I do makes a difference."
   "Something bad always happens to me."
   "It'll never work."
   "I knew this would happen."
   "There's always something."

A positive outlook does not mean being a Pollyanna who believes that everything is wonderful when it is not. Nor does it mean burying your head in the sand like an ostrich. A positive outlook means looking reality straight in the eye and realistically assessing what you can achieve in the situation.

Here are some suggestions to help you attain and maintain a positive outlook.

1. Look at problems as opportunities. Write out the problem. Now, rewrite it, and phrase it as an opportunity. Here's an example.

   Problem: I am the team leader for a group of people who could not care less about the goals of this team.

   Opportunity: I am the team leader who can use my people skills and abilities to inspire my team to achieve a common goal. In doing this, I am making myself more promotable.

2. Write out the steps you will take to take advantage of this opportunity. You might want to go back to your self-worth list and check off any experiences or abilities you have that will help you directly achieve your goal.

3. Avoid gripe sessions. It's easy to get into the "ain't it awful" mode. Instead, focus on something positive. Move the group to a positive outlook by modeling the behavior you expect. Relax, smile, lower your voice, breathe deeply, respond slowly. Your subliminal message is that you believe you can handle this situation. It hasn't made you nervous, upset or emotional.

4. Change the messages that you give yourself. Try some of the following phrases:

   "I succeed at whatever I put my mind to."
   "It can be done."
   "I'll find a way."

"Everyone and everything I encounter teaches me something."

"I can make a difference."

It requires courage and strength of mind to face whatever life brings you and to find the good, the positive and the opportunities that lie there. However, a positive mental outlook is one of the most readily identifiable qualities of a leader. People naturally respond to someone who expects the best from them and from the relationship.

CORE BELIEF FOUR: PERSONAL SECURITY

When you have a strong belief in your personal security, you feel that you are part of the big picture of life. You are willing to take some risks because you feel secure in your place in the universe. You are able to give up control when needed and trust others to support you.

What is your belief about your personal security? Think about your answers to the following questions.

1. Do you feel all alone in life?

2. Do you think that people will take advantage of you if you give them a chance?

3. Do you believe that you have to look out for yourself constantly because you can't trust anyone?

4. Do you need to be in control all the time? Do you feel panicky when you lose control?

5. Do you share your successes with others?

As you answer these questions, you might feel that personal security sounds more like childish trust. If you see this world as a dog-eat-dog situation, then you may have trouble dealing with the idea that you can let go and move through life boldly and freely, secure in the trust you place in others.

Leaders with a low sense of personal security tend to be dictatorial. They seldom see themselves as part of a team. In fact, they usually feel isolated and set apart from the rest of their team members. As a result, they move through life with caution and fear.

Creating a sense of personal security for yourself takes time. You will need to focus on your place in the universe and learn to trust the people in that universe. Here are some suggestions.

1. Begin to find your place in the universe. Consider how you fit into your family, your company, your profession, your community, your nation and this world.

2. See yourself as a member of your team. See your team members as fellow brothers and sisters in the universe.

3. Spend your time generously with others, listening to and encouraging them whenever possible.

4. Establish links with those around you. Call a friend, bring a gift to your spouse, kiss a child, spend time with a relative, volunteer at a local hospital. Begin to give parts of yourself to others.

5. Slowly begin to trust people. Give them opportunities to support you. Believe in the inherent goodness of the universe and allow that goodness to flow to you.

Personal security allows you, as a team leader, to enjoy the best from your team. It also allows you to expect your team to support you and enhance your position as the leader.

CORE BELIEF FIVE: ATTITUDE TOWARD CHANGE

Most of us have grown up believing that for life to be secure and stable, nothing should change. This belief has created the illusion that stability is a law of nature. In fact, quite the reverse is true, however. Nature is continuously in a state of change — growing, evolving, expanding, breaking down, dying and renewing. We are in a similar state of change.

Do you get upset when something unexpected occurs? Are you anxious when circumstances change? For many, change is threatening. How do you feel about change?

1. Do you resist change and find security in having things remain the same?

2. Do you have a rigidly defined daily routine? Do you go to work the same way every day, read the same newspapers, watch the same television programs, eat the same foods and see the same people?

3. Do you feel that you have gone as far as you can in your profession?

4. Do you often use excuses to avoid making changes?

    "I'm too old (young, tired, inexperienced, over-qualified, short, tall, fat, unhealthy, tied-down) to try (start, learn, begin, stop, take on, give up) that."

5. Do you feel that your life is completely predictable?

The introduction to this handbook pointed out that organizational hierarchies are changing rapidly. Like it or not, you are caught up in these changes. Becoming a team leader is a profound change in the way you always have regarded your status in the organization. If this change creates fear and anxiety, the resulting stress will affect how well you perform as a team leader. Being able to "go with the flow" is one of the most valuable assets a team leader can have. You can learn how to embrace the changes around you and use them positively. Try some of the following ideas.

1. Break the daily and weekly routine that you have set. Try something new every day for a week: a new route to work, a new book, a new television program, a new group for coffee, even a new way of handling your daily work routine.

2. Get in tune with the changes going on in the world around you. Attend seminars or lectures on change. Read some of the latest books written by gurus of change.

3. Make a list of all the things that have changed in your professional life in the last year. Look at each item and determine whether you felt threatened by the change or whether you saw it as an opportunity. If you felt threatened, jot down some ways in which the change could be an opportunity for you. Do the same for the changes you are experiencing today.

As a team leader, you have a unique opportunity to participate in one of the most profound changes in the organizational environment today. You can be on the cutting edge of empowerment and responsibility in your organization. If you embrace it and use it positively, this change can be an essential ingredient in your career success.

When you have examined your core beliefs, you may discover the reasons for some of your discomfort as a team leader. Remember, this discomfort, in whatever guise, will transfer to your team members. Before you can empower your team members to participate fully and take responsibility for their parts of the team goal, you must empower yourself to change the core beliefs that limit you.

SELF-EMPOWERED REPROGRAMMING

Before you can change or reprogram yourself, you need to understand how your core belief program works.

If you ever have operated a computer of any kind — word processor, VCR, videogame — you'll find it easy to understand your own programming. There are basically three levels to a computer program. Level one is the actual program written by a computer programmer in a language understood only by a computer. If you were to see this program printed out, it would look like a meaningless jumble of symbols, numbers and letters, something like this:

*^^756$ 03As## 2Y# 44$$%XCC *&#09

At level two, the program is triggered by an outside source. For example, if you are playing a videogame, you must "boot" the game with pre-set commands or instructions or by hitting a certain key on the computer. That is the trigger. Once the program has been triggered, it automatically moves to level three. The program "runs." That is, you see visible evidence that the program is under way. The video creations move on the screen.

Using a word-processing program for your example, the analogy works the same way. First, the program is written; you trigger it by entering a password or keystroke; then you are able to use the program for what it has been programmed to do.

SUPER-CONSCIOUS, SUBCONSCIOUS AND CONSCIOUS

Your mind works in much the same way. There is a written program at level 1 in the SUPER-CONSCIOUS. This is where your basic core beliefs lie. When something triggers this program, level 2 or the SUBCONSCIOUS takes over. At level 3 or the CONSCIOUS mind, you see the visible results. For example, on a purely physical level, you have a level 1 program that tells you when you feel pain. Put your hand in fire. That certainly will trigger the program. Then level 2, the subconscious part of your brain that controls automatic actions, kicks in and sets up the reflexes that will move your hand from the fire. At level 3, you pull your hand out of the fire. All this happens in an instant, so you would call it an "automatic reaction."

WHY MAKING A CONSCIOUS CHANGE DOESN'T WORK

When you are dealing with any habit, whether it is biting your nails or reacting to a belief, you must realize that the program cannot be changed at level 3 only. A level 3 change lasts only as long as you CONSCIOUSLY can enforce it. One moment of inattention and levels 1 and 2 override the change. Again, if you ever have operated a word-processing program on a computer, you know that you can make superficial changes to the program, such as formatting with double spacing. But every time you reactivate the program, you also must remember to put in the change. Otherwise, the program automatically reverts back to its original setting.

HOW DID THE ORIGINAL PROGRAM GET THERE IN THE FIRST PLACE?

I'm sure that you have no recollection of writing a program in your super-conscious that tells you to react according to particular beliefs whenever you are confronted by certain places, situations, persons or things. That's because you didn't write the original program. As you learned earlier, other people wrote your original belief programs.

Your mother, your older brother, your Sunday school teacher, your school crossing guard, your best friend's father, Great Aunt Martha, Cousin Bob, the school principal, the lady in the library, the bus driver, Mr. Brown across the street and Mrs. Jones at the drugstore — they all had something to say about you and your life. Many of their comments, both good and bad, simply passed you by. But some comments, particularly if they were echoed by others, often repeated or believed by you, became a part of your automatic belief program. Without you being aware of it, a program was written that would affect how you deal with many areas of your life, long after the original "writers" were gone.

There is yet another level of subtlety to your belief program. Unlike a computerized program, the language used in your belief program is easily understood. And just to make sure that the messages are loud and clear, the belief program sends them out in the "first person" format. Thus, the messages become:

> "I don't have any choices in life."
> "I don't deserve this success."
> "I have to struggle to survive."
> "I can't trust anyone but myself."
> "I can't handle change."

The program messages are sent out by an inner voice that points out all your failures and weaknesses. Each time you use negative behavior, you agree with the program message. Each time you agree, you reinforce the message for the next time.

To make a change in a core belief, you need to know what is happening at level 1. To do this, take any one of your inner-voice messages and work with it to reach level 1. Simply ask, "Why?" For example, if your message is, "I don't have any choices in life," repeat the message and then ask, "Why?" Your inner dialogue might go something like this:

> "I don't have any choices in life."
>   "Why?"
> "Because I have to do what is expected of me."
>   "Why?"
> "Because others expect me to do certain things."
>   "Why?"

"Because I always have fulfilled their expectations."
    "Why?"
"Because I think it's my duty."
    "Why?"
"Because no one else will do these things."
    "Why?"

Keep on going until you reach a core belief. Perhaps in this dialogue you might discover that your core belief is that you have to do what people want you to do or they won't like you anymore. From there, you can examine the belief for truth. Do you really believe this? What experiences have backed up this belief? What would happen if you choose to substitute another belief for this one?

By working with your level 1 super-conscious, you can begin to change your core beliefs so they will enhance your life and your leadership.

3

THE MANAGEMENT STYLE THAT EMPOWERS OTHERS

Assuming you've worked through your core values in Chapter Two, you should feel much better about your own empowerment. Your core beliefs now are working for you, rather than against you. Here are the reasons why.

1. You feel confident that you can take responsibility for the success of the team.

2. You have accepted your right to be a team leader.

3. You express your feelings of self-worth through your body language and your positive statements.

4. You see each team meeting as an opportunity for you to use your skills and abilities.

5. You trust your team members and consider yourself one of them.

6. You are excited about being part of the changes that are taking place in your organization.

Now you are ready to assume your position as a team leader. It's time to call another meeting.

Once again, the meeting is set for 9 a.m. This time you start rounding up people early, and by 9:02 a.m. everyone is on deck.

Remembering your resolve to match your actions to your core beliefs, you compliment those who come on time. You sit up straight, look people in the eye, talk positively and watch out for any self-defeating phrases. In short, you do everything right. But, no one is acting as if he or she is empowered. No one makes any suggestions. No one gives an opinion. No one responds to any of your questions.

At 9:45 a.m., you regretfully end the meeting. Inwardly, you sigh with relief that the ordeal is over — again. What went wrong this time? You may have changed inside, but nothing else has changed. No one is any more empowered than at the last meeting.

EMPOWERING YOUR TEAM

Empowerment means three things:

1. Being enabled

2. Being committed

3. Being productive

ENABLING YOUR TEAM

If you take these three components of empowerment and apply them to your team, you first need to enable team members. Here's how.

- Give them permission to be participative members of the team.

- Create opportunities for them to express their thoughts, ideas and opinions.

- Encourage them to listen and give feedback to each other.

You suspect that there is a lot more to enabling a team than just changing your own core beliefs and attitudes. Your actions, which give both overt and subliminal messages, provide the foundation. You build upon this foundation of actions by using a proven method of leadership.

THE PARTICIPATIVE MANAGEMENT STYLE

One of the best ways to enable a team is to use a participative management style. Participative management stems from the idea of allowing employees to have input into the decision-making process. Although the idea has been around for quite a while, its popularity has waxed and waned. Some managers think it simply means to be nice to their employees. Others see it as being sensitive to feelings and needs. Some believe it means asking for help. Yet other participative management proponents seem to think it means having lots of meetings!

That's probably why your first impulse as a team leader was to call a meeting. Instinctively you knew that your team leadership style would include components of participative management. Calling a meeting, therefore, seemed a good place to start.

When you think about the two meetings with your team, you begin to suspect that while you may have wanted to use a participative leadership style, you fell back on the more familiar autocratic style. This is the style that you've seen in the old hierarchical relationships, the kind that you're most familiar with.

Here are some of the characteristics of the autocratic style that you may have displayed during your first two meetings.

1.   Communication was mostly downward. You did all the talking. No one responded to you.

2. You used your power position as team leader to ensure that everyone knew you were in charge. You set the agenda. You called the meeting.

3. No only did you do all the talking, but you told people what the boss expected, what you expected and what they were to do.

4. People tend to do things because they have to. There was no discussion as you handed out assignments and responsibilities.

5. People put in their time. Your team members came to the meeting only because your position as team leader forced them to attend. They didn't bring any enthusiasm or energy with them.

6. Any visible energy seemed to decrease. If anything, there was even less energy and enthusiasm at the second team meeting than at the first.

This isn't what you wanted. You wanted a team that really acted like a team. So how do you become a participative leader?

THE PARTICIPATIVE LEADER IN ACTION

First, you need to help your team members learn how to communicate upward, downward and horizontally. The lack of response from the team is a good indication that communication needs to be fostered carefully. There are several ways you can do this.

1. Describe the situation from your point of view and ask for feedback.

   "I think that we have some problems with scheduling. So far, we haven't been able to get everyone together on the same day at the same time. I think we need to take everyone's schedules into consideration before we set the next meeting. As I see it, some of us will have to make a few schedule changes to accommodate the rest of the group. What do you think?"

   Reacting in this way, you do not imply that anyone was wrong for missing a meeting. However, you do recognize a problem and the need for everyone to have some input in the solution.

2. Treat everyone equally.

   "I know that some of you are tied up with computer time-sharing, but because we're all in this together, let's cover every angle."

   No one is made to feel that his concerns are less important than anyone else's, regardless of status or job assignment.

3. Maintain an open attitude.

   "So far, I've just arbitrarily assigned a meeting time, but I would appreciate your ideas and input. Does anyone have any thoughts on how we can get together on this?"

Express an interest in a shared approach and
solicit input from the team members.

4. Acknowledge the problem, but focus on a
   solution.

   "I can see that we've got a problem here
   because everyone has different schedules and
   assignment responsibilities. However, I'm sure
   that we can collectively come up with a
   solution we can all live with."

   Too often, leaders ignore a problem or belittle
   its importance. This makes team members
   reluctant to be seen as "nit-pickers" or as
   "problem-oriented." Instead, acknowledge that
   there is a problem and then encourage the
   group to work together on a solution.

5. Be sensitive to people's feelings and needs.

   "I can see that you're feeling squeezed, Fred.
   This meeting must seem like just one more
   thing that you've got to put into your schedule.
   Is there some way the team can help you?"

   Being empathetic with other people's problems
   signals your willingness to accept their feelings
   at face value and to work with them on their
   problems.

POSITIONAL VS. PERSONAL POWER

One of the reasons why team members are reluctant to open up and communicate is that they see the team leader in a power position. Although the team leader does not have any real authority — he can't demand obedience — the habit of allowing the person in power to make all the decisions is strongly ingrained in people who have worked in a traditional organizational hierarchy. When you act as if you have the authority and power to make demands on your team, members correspondingly will treat your demands just as they do when they have little or no input: They will give lip service but no enthusiasm or energy.

What kind of power should the leader of a team demonstrate? Personal power! Personal power is not conferred on you by higher authorities but comes from your own skills, abilities, experience and actions. Personal power allows you to use your people skills to create upward, downward and horizontal communication among your team members.

In other words, personal power is a kind of people-oriented, quiet power. You see yourself in the position of helping team members use their own skills, abilities and experiences to contribute to the success of the team. It's a long way from the old positional power role of telling people what to do!

Using your personal power rather than your positional power greatly enables the team to work toward its goals. Here are some practical suggestions for using personal power as a team leader.

1. Encourage the group to work together on
    decision-making. Strive for consensus, in which
    each group member has an opportunity to
    participate.

2. Allow members of the group to have some say
    in assignments. Sometimes their assessments of
    their own abilities are more accurate than
    yours, and often they will share tasks and work
    together if given the opportunity.

3. Give the team the responsibility, as a unit, for
    reviewing and evaluating its progress on the
    tasks.

RESPONSIBILITY AND THE PARTICIPATIVE LEADER

When you were appointed team leader, you made a
number of decisions about your responsibilities
because you are the one who will be held accountable
for the success or failure of the team. You nominated
yourself as being responsible for everything!

But look at responsibility from your team members'
viewpoint by putting yourself in their positions. Have
you ever been in a situation where you had no
responsibility at all? Perhaps you went to a meeting
with no agenda, and the leader let everyone talk on
and on and on! Or you may have attended a seminar
in which you watched the presenter make some
serious errors and could do nothing about them.
Maybe you were in a position where the orders came
down from "on high," and you had to follow them.

Remember how you felt in those kinds of situations? Helpless. Frustrated. Angry. Apathetic. Listless. Uninvolved. Where was your energy level? Hitting zero!

That's exactly what happens with your team members when you take on all the responsibility. They just sit there and let it all happen or not happen, as the case may be. No wonder they lack enthusiasm.

The best way to ensure enthusiasm, involvement and energy in a team is to allow the members to take some of the responsibility for their project. "But what if they screw up or let me down? I'm the one who will ultimately be responsible!"

True. But there is a point when all leaders must rely on their core beliefs — they are part of a team and they can trust their fellow team members to support them.

How do you encourage shared responsibility in your team?

1. Set up assignments that require the input and cooperation of several members.

2. Share all information.

3. Show your team members how their particular tasks are part of the whole-group task.

4. Allow members of the team to share their skills and knowledge with each other. Encourage "cross training" within the team.

5. Link rewards to group performance, not individual performance.

Now you have some concrete ideas on how to enable your team by becoming a participative leader. It's time to call another meeting! But before you do, reprogram yourself to become that participative leader.

USING SELF-EMPOWERMENT TO BECOME A PARTICIPATIVE MANAGER

To become an effective participative manager, you must examine your own beliefs about the role of a manager. You may find that your beliefs are incompatible with the actions of a participative manager. When this happens, your actions may be participative, but those underlying beliefs will give a subliminal message that says otherwise.

One of the best ways to uncover your beliefs about a manager's role is to look at your role models. Think about a person that you admire professionally. List the qualities that make him an effective manager. To see how you have used this person as a role model, perform these two steps.

STEP 1   Next to each quality, put an A for authoritative style or a P for participative style.

STEP 2   Check off the qualities you try to copy in your own management style.

Now, make another list. Start out with the heading, "A Good Manager Should..." Think of everything you've ever believed that a good manager "should" do or be. When you have completed your list, perform the two steps again.

Finally, draw up a third list. This time, the list will have two columns. Column one is headed: "My Strengths as a Manager;" column two: "My Weaknesses as a Manager." Take some time with these lists. Make sure that you don't sell yourself short on the strengths list. Then perform the two steps again. But in step two ask yourself, "Which strengths and weaknesses affect my current leadership role?"

A pattern of your beliefs about management style should emerge. People usually copy those whom they admire if they find themselves in a similar situation. If you admire a certain leader, you probably will use his leadership style if you are cast in a leadership role. Your first list will tell you whether you are copying an authoritarian or a participative management style.

We also have beliefs that are expressed in "should" statements. Such "should" statements are sometimes incompatible with our actions. For example, you may have a statement that says you should lose weight to be healthy, yet you consistently make food choices that prevent weight loss, such as eating fried chicken instead of broiled.

In your professional life, your "should" statements about being a good manager will show you what your underlying beliefs are. You may think that a good manager should be open to ideas from the team, yet your actions may indicate you do not welcome ideas other than your own.

When you look at your list of strengths and weaknesses, you may discover that your weaknesses lie in the area of participative management, while your strengths are those of an authoritarian manager. If this is the case, then you need to begin a program of self-improvement by reading books, attending seminars, talking to others, practicing new skills and taking courses. All of these skills will help you turn participative weaknesses into leadership strengths.

The following self-evaluation also will help you determine in which areas you need to empower yourself to change your management style.

A. Team Communication

   1. Do you feel uncomfortable asking for feedback from your team for fear that it may be negative?

   2. Do you find it difficult to treat everyone on the team equally?

   3. Do you find yourself relying on some members more than others?

   4. Do you give some team members more responsibility than others?

   5. Do you tend to listen more to some team members than to others?

6. Do you avoid addressing how your team members feel about some issues?

7. Do you avoid bringing up problems because you don't want to give a negative impression?

8. Do you tend to ignore problems and hope they will resolve themselves?

9. Do you see discussion about a problem as a time waster?

B. Power

1. Do you feel anxious when team members do not treat you with the respect that you feel your position warrants?

2. Do you often suspect that team members will select only "easy" assignments if they are given the power to choose their own?

3. Do you dislike spending the time required for the group to achieve consensus?

C. Responsibility

1. Do you feel uncomfortable relinquishing any responsibility to the group?

2. Do you prefer to parcel out information to the group only as required?

3. Do you usually reward individuals for
    performance, rather than the group as a whole?

These questions will help you pinpoint the areas
where you may need to work on your participative
management style. For each question, a "no" answer
indicates a need for self-improvement.

Try not to see yourself as having the "wrong"
management style, but rather as being "on the way" to
becoming a participative manager. Remember that
everything you do is a learning experience, including
any actions you already have taken as the leader of
your team.

Set up a plan of action for your self-improvement.
Based on what you have found out about your
participative management style, review this chapter
and make notes that will help improve your style.

MY PERSONAL ACTION PLAN

I WILL BEGIN DOING:

1.

2.

3.

I WILL STOP DOING:

1.

2.

3.

Now, just as you must empower yourself to begin building a house, you also must empower yourself to take the actions listed in your plan. Writing them down is a good start. You have given your subconscious a powerful message that it will use to run your action program at your next team meeting.

4

CREATING COMMITMENT IN YOUR TEAM

There is a definite difference in the atmosphere of your next team meeting. As you actively encourage your team members to communicate, making it clear that you are not using positional power to get what you want, things begin to happen.

The team comes up with a meeting schedule that everyone likes and is willing to try. The work assignments are realigned, and in some cases several team members take on an assignment as a group. In fact, one team member even offers to teach another how to do a complex function that will greatly improve the quality of the work.

The meeting doesn't end until nearly 10 a.m. Someone even thanks you for a good meeting!

You are confident that your team now is enabled and that the second phase of empowerment — commitment — surely will follow.

Unfortunately, the next meeting tells you that there is still a long way to go! Although each team member is positive about the team function, the actual assignments are far from being completed. Several team members say things like, "I just didn't get around to it this week," "Something else came up and I had to drop this work," "I didn't think there was any urgency in getting this done," "I ran out of time," and "I wasn't sure how to do this, so I left it."

Team members may be enabled, but they certainly are not committed to their tasks. You feel like you are spinning your wheels, accomplishing little or nothing.

To help your team become committed, you need to provide it with three elements:

1. Direction

2. Resources

3. Support

DIRECTION

Let's start with the most important element. If a team has no direction, it has no purpose, no goals and no clear expectations. It has no real reason for being. A consciously chosen and clearly articulated direction puts to use the talents and abilities of your team members and commits them personally to the task at hand.

It's the same thing as bringing together a group of your friends with the clear intention of packing food boxes for the local food bank. The purpose: packing boxes. The goal: packing a certain number of boxes in the given time. The results: needy people will receive food this month. Overall, your group has a direction: to help alleviate hunger among the disadvantaged. There may be some other reasons, but your main direction and purpose provide a practical, common vision for your group to follow.

Direction is created from the purpose for the team, the goals of the team and the key results expected from the team. It does not come from the purpose/goal/results that your boss handed to you when you were appointed team leader. The direction of your team may end up the same as your boss' purpose/goal/results, but it has to start out as a direction that the team creates. Part of the reason why so many teams are uncommitted is that someone else decided what their direction would be. Lack of personal input saps the team's energy and enthusiasm. As a result, there is little commitment.

You've probably already told your team members the purpose/goal/results that your boss told you. Obviously, it hasn't fired their commitment. You need to help your team create its own direction. Start by formulating a purpose for the team.

PURPOSE

Try asking the question, "Why are we here as a team?" You'll probably hear a lot of responses that have little to do with purpose, especially if you've fostered open communication among team members.

Some typical responses might be: "Because the boss told us to get together." "Because someone has to do this job." "Because the company has some new idea about putting people together in teams." "Because you called a meeting."

Can you hear the lack of commitment in those responses? In each case, someone else has made the decision for the team. The team members remain uninvolved.

Don't give up. Try brainstorming with your team members. Get them to think of the things that this group does particularly well. You can spark their thinking with questions like these:

- What can the team do that no one else in the organization can? Where does the team fit into the overall organization?

- What can the team contribute to the organization?

- How can the team enhance the career goals of each member? What does each member want out of the team?

- What would the company lose if the team disbanded?

Write down the answers and plan time for discussion. Then begin to put together a rough statement of purpose. Don't worry about getting it exactly right. At this point, you're just putting together something that the team can work with.

You might come up with something like this: "We are here to provide the best quality control system in our industry, based upon the extensive expertise of the team members, using the latest computer technology and sharing our ideas and skills with each other while maintaining a less than 2 percent error margin." From this statement, you can begin to distill your team's essential purpose.

Work with your group, making sure that each team member feels that he has a responsibility to create this statement of purpose. Try to elicit responses from every member. Your finished statement should be clear, easily understood and agreed upon by all members of the team.

Your final statement of purpose might be: "Our team is here to provide a computerized quality control mechanism that sets the standards within our industry." You'll notice that some of the earlier ideas are missing. You'll be able to include those as other components of your team's direction.

GOALS

Now that you have a purpose, you can begin to work on the goals that will move you toward achieving the purpose. A goal is different from a purpose because it is specific, measurable and has a beginning and an end. When you go back to your original ideas for the purpose, you'll find some of the goals for your team. One goal could be "to reduce all errors by a margin of less than 2 percent." Another might be "to teach all team members how to use computer programs for quality control."

Spend some time setting these goals because they will become part of the specific work assignments for the team members. In fact, you may find that members will volunteer to work on particular goals that interest them.

RESULTS

Now you need to find the results component of the team's direction. Again you'll need to lead your team in a brainstorming session. Try asking questions like these:

- How will we know that we are fulfilling our purpose?

- How will we know that we are moving in the right direction?

- What will tell us that we have met our goals?

You might hear responses such as: "When errors are less than 2 percent." "When other companies ask our advice on quality control." "When each of us is able to perform every control function."

With these three components — purpose, goals and results — you now have a direction for your team. Direction is more than a device for creating commitment within the team. It also serves some practical purposes.

1. Direction provides a yardstick for team members to measure their assignments.

2. Direction gives the team a context in which to make decisions regarding its work.

3. Direction acts as a motivator and an energizer that commits members to work together.

RESOURCES

The second element required to create commitment in your team is resources. "Resources" mean many things: training, information, tools, materials, facilities, time and money. You may or may not be in a position to provide any or all of these. However, your team needs resources to be able to fulfill the expectations that are written down in its direction.

This is one area where you can use positional power. As the team leader, it's up to you to approach management and ask for the resources that your team needs.

If you are unable to obtain the necessary resources, put the responsibility back on your team members. Let them work on alternative ways to achieve the direction of the team. Can they share resources? Can they double up on assignments? Can they fill in for one another? If members see this as a challenge to their creativity and resourcefulness rather than an insurmountable problem, they will work together to "show" people that they can do it. In many cases, this kind of shared responsibility fosters a sense of belonging and togetherness that characterizes an empowered team. The team's commitment to "making it work" grows.

SUPPORT

Finally, the team needs support to be committed. This area is initially your responsibility.

Tom Peters, the author of *Thriving on Chaos*, proposes a wonderful prescription for the kind of support a team needs. He calls it "listen/celebrate/recognize."

Let's start with listening. Millions of words have been written on how to talk to people, but few tell you how to listen. Yet, to listen to someone — *really listen* — is one of the most effective ways to empower that person.

Listening is more than just not talking. Listening means focusing your complete attention on the other person. That is, not doing anything else: not reading, not eating, not doodling or not looking around the room. It means looking at another person squarely in the eyes and responding to what he is saying with the appropriate facial and body movements. Listening is hard work.

As a team leader, it is your responsibility to model the kind of listening you expect of the other members of the team. Once your team members know that you really listen to them, they will begin to share some of their problems, expectations, successes and failures with you. More importantly, they will follow your listening model and begin to listen to each other.

Your response to listening also should be a model for the team. Respond with empathy. You can show that you are listening by summarizing what you have heard, but you also must go beyond the words by making an empathetic statement such as, "I sense that you're feeling very frustrated."

When Peters talks about "celebrating" as a function of supporting the team, he means small, celebratory events that mark a job well done. Pick up doughnuts and bring them to the next meeting. Arrange to have a meeting at everyone's favorite luncheon spot. Ask the boss to attend a meeting and make a special presentation. Get baseball caps for everyone. Order a balloon-o-gram!

Recognition is also important. You might want to make it a habit during each meeting to single out those who have achieved their assigned goals. Name names! Better still, post names on the bulletin board. Let everyone know when someone has done well. Hand-written thank-you notes are still one of the best and least expensive ways for a team leader to express recognition.

Recognition not only makes people feel that their effort was worthwhile, it also creates commitment to keep up the effort.

BEFORE THE NEXT MEETING

You can work on empowering your team to be committed to the task ahead before you call another meeting. Start by talking individually to the team members. Take a few moments and find out how they feel about the direction of the team. Ask them to begin thinking about purpose, goals and results. Let them know that their input is important to you. This is a good time to practice your listening skills as well!

Be sure to include empathy statements with your listening responses. Listen beyond the words. What is this person feeling about this situation? Are there any hidden agendas?

This is also a good time to find out what resources team members feel are needed to accomplish their tasks. Let them know you will go to bat for them with the boss.

Be prepared to share with the team the results of your efforts. Ask them for their help and input on this challenge.

Try to find something to celebrate — perhaps just surviving another week — and plan to do it at the next meeting. Send out a few thank-you notes.

You are now well on your way to having a team that is empowered.

EMPOWERING YOURSELF TOWARD COMMITMENT

Before you can lead your team to commitment, you also must be personally committed to your role as team leader.

You need a direction. The first step is to create your own *purpose*. Just as you wanted your team to respond to the question, "Why are we here?", you need to answer that question for yourself. Use the same questions that you used for the team (page 44), only substitute your name for "the team" and you for "the members." The answers will tell you your purpose for being the team leader.

Then, write down all the things you will need to do to achieve this purpose. These are your *goals*. Make sure that they are specific, have a beginning and an end, and are measurable.

Finally, articulate the expected *results*. Ask yourself, "What will tell me that I have achieved my purpose?"

For example, one of your purposes could be "to enable my team."

A goal to achieve this purpose could be to set up assignments that require input and cooperation from several members of the team. You may choose a specific assignment, a specific time frame for its completion and the specific team members who could take on this task. You will know that you have achieved your purpose when your team works together to complete the assignment. Together the three components create a direction for your leadership.

To move in this direction, you need to consider the resources that you will need. Do you need training? Do you need more information? Do you need special tools or materials? Do you need specific facilities? Do you need time or money? Pinpoint the necessary resources now and draw up a plan to obtain them. Without appropriate resources, your direction may be unattainable.

Finally, just as your team requires support to be committed to its task, you also require support. But who is going to give you that support? The answer lies within yourself.

LISTEN

Listen to your inner voice. What are you saying to yourself? Are you giving yourself positive reinforcement, or are you allowing the "enemy within" to undermine all your efforts? If you need to, go back and reprogram your inner voice.

CELEBRATE

Do you reward yourself when you feel good about your actions? Just as your team needs small celebrations, so do you! Take yourself out to lunch. Buy yourself a small gift. Indulge a taste passion. Go to a movie. These small celebrations in your own life empower you to move on. One of the hardest things to do is to reward yourself.

RECOGNIZE

Recognize your own personal achievements. Instead of focusing on what you have done wrong, begin to look at what you have done right. Keep a scorecard. No one else needs to know what it means, but you'll feel a wonderful sense of satisfaction every time you give yourself points for achieving your goals.

If someone comments favorably on your leadership, accept the compliment. Don't brush it off with a remark like, "Oh, it was nothing." Allow yourself to bask a little, to enjoy the feeling of being OK. After all, you would do the same thing for your team members.

5

WHAT STIFLES
TEAM CREATIVITY?

Remember that empowerment for your team members
means that they are:

- enabled

- committed

- productive

By enabling yourself, you have enabled your team.

By giving your team direction, resources and support,
you have created commitment within the team. But
can you have a team that is enabled and committed,
but not productive? The answer is yes.

By its definition, "productivity" is an elusive quality that does not necessarily result from being enabled and/or committed. According to the *Webster Dictionary,* productivity is "yielding or furnishing results, benefits or profits; yielding or devoted to the satisfaction of wants or the creation of utilities."

Productivity goes beyond doing just enough to get by. It means breaking through old patterns and behaviors, expanding limits and possibilities and creating new answers to old problems. The productive team is a creative team.

As usual, before you can empower your team to think creatively, you first must empower yourself to be creative. How do you limit your creativity? By creating a set of "don'ts" to guide your every move.

Four don'ts limit the creativity of you and your team.

DON'T MAKE MISTAKES

1. Do you tend to remember your mistakes more than your successes?

2. Do you worry about making a mistake when you have to try something that you've never done before?

3. Do you think about what can go wrong before you think about what can go right?

4. Do you dislike having to learn something by "trial and error?"

From the moment when you ran home and proudly announced that you scored 99 out of 100 on your test, you no doubt received the message that you shouldn't make mistakes. Your test paper probably had one red check mark on it, rather than 99 "correct answer" marks. "What happened to the other point?" was the response to your news. Unfortunately, we live in a society that looks for mistakes and typically points out what is wrong rather than what is right.

"Don't make mistakes" is a message you carry with you into adulthood. Living and working in an adult world, you still try to avoid mistakes. You cautiously feel your way through each day, avoiding any risks that might lead to failure. You learn that the safest way to avoid mistakes is to stick with the tried and true.

Being appointed team leader probably caused you a great deal of anxiety because you feared making a mistake. This kind of thinking puts your creativity under lock and key and, consequently, you do the same thing to your team. You don't want members making any mistakes either!

Think about mistakes. Mistakes are how you learn. If you never made a mistake, you'd still be lying on your back in your baby crib. It was through trial and error that you learned to roll over, sit up, stand up, crawl and eventually walk. Everything you learn in life comes from the trial-and-error process. In the same way, your learning comes from your mistakes.

Just getting this far with your team members has had its share of trial and error. Remember your first disastrous meeting with them? You came away feeling that you had made a mistake. But you didn't make the same mistake the next time or the next or the next.

To move beyond "good enough" to "excellent," and from "adequate" to "above expectations," you need to give your team members permission to make mistakes. Encourage them to try some new, innovative approaches to their problems. Let them know that mistakes are OK and that they are part of the learning process.

Then stand back and watch what happens!

DON'T WASTE TIME

1. Do you feel uncomfortable when you have nothing specific that you need to do?

2. Are you frustrated when people get off the subject in meetings?

3. Do you try to use every minute in a structured way?

4. Do you consider yourself to be a better time manager than most of the people you know?

Somewhere in your life, there was probably someone urging you to "use your time wisely." Unfortunately, that person didn't tell you what "wisely" meant. In today's business world, wisely is construed to mean only things pertaining to business and getting things done. Anything else is considered a waste of time.

Consider your own attitude toward meetings. Don't you feel resentful and angry when you suspect that a meeting has been a complete waste of your time? The leader did not keep the meeting on track. He allowed people to wander off the topic, talk about non-agenda items or go on interminably about the same subject. The leader was not in control.

When you plan your own meetings, do you agonize over what is worthwhile and what is a time waster? In fact, there are no time wasters in a team meeting if you have planned for the item as part of the agenda, know the purpose for its inclusion and know how to control it. Therefore, some kind of warm-up exercise is not a time waster as long as you control it. Neither is reporting on previous activities as long as you limit the allotted time.

However, your don't-waste-time attitude really kicks in when someone goes astray from the planned agenda. The agenda that you set is your way of ensuring that you retain control. An off-agenda item sets off an alarm in your head — you are losing control of the meeting! Even worse, you're sure that this will be a waste of time!

A rigidly controlled agenda is one of the best ways to stifle creativity. Any lateral thinking — thinking that uses free association to move from one idea to the next rather than logical structure — is squelched.

Here's how it happens. Your agenda item calls for a discussion on ways and means to get reports to all team members as quickly as possible. The usual methods are brought up: deadlines, multiple copies of everything and electronic mail. These methods have been tried, but team members still arrive at the meeting unprepared.

Then, a team member starts to talk about the problems with his car pool. The talk moves to the specifics of personalities in the car pool, and you sense the growing frustration in the rest of the team as the discussion goes far off the topic. But is it really off the topic? It is your job as team leader to foster the creative thinking that may be the reason behind the off-topic discussion. Perhaps this team member's lateral thinking process was triggered when he heard words like "schedule," "deadlines" or "responsibility." The car pool came to mind. Why? Perhaps there are similarities between the car pool and your reporting problems. The answer to your team's particular problem could lie in that similarity.

Before the team member wanders too far off the topic, find out why he made the mental jump from reporting to car pools. Ask him, "What made you think of your car pool when we were talking about our reporting problems?" Often, we are unaware of why our brains make a lateral jump until we address the topic directly.

"Well, we had the same kind of trouble getting everyone to do his part. People arrived late, forgot it was their turn or failed to let us know if they weren't coming."

"How did you solve it?"

"We appointed a different person each week to be responsible for the car pool. That person called the rest, reminded them who was driving, made sure they were going to be on time and found out if anyone wouldn't be available."

"How could this work for something like our reporting system?"

With this question you're on your way to fostering creativity within your team! The secret is to forget about "time wasting" and presume that there is a creative process involved. Tap into that process by guiding the discussion. If there really is no parallel between the car pool and the reporting system and the team member is just meandering, bring your team members back on topic and move on.

DON'T PUT THINGS OFF — DO THEM NOW!

1. Do you make lists of things that must be done today and feel guilty if you don't get them all done?

2. Do you give yourself rigid deadlines in which to solve problems?

3. Do you get angry with yourself when you don't come up with a solution within your deadline?

4. Do you push yourself to get it done NOW?

Society is conditioned to be afraid of the word "procrastination." You bring this fear into your role as group leader by continually urging your team to "do it now." Deadlines are set; discussions must come to a conclusion; decisions must be made at once. There is no doubt that limiting procrastination gets things done, but at the same time, not allowing any procrastination sometimes hampers the creative process.

Part of this creative process is that magical thing called "insight." Insight includes the sudden inspiration, the off-the-wall idea and the "ah hah" moment. Insight is the result of three steps:

1. Focus
2. Recreate
3. Oscillate

First, focus on the task. Pour all your energy into looking at every aspect of the task in front of you. Discuss it, think about it and define it. This part is easy for teams. It's what they do best.

This is usually the time that you, as team leader, call for closure. "Let's not procrastinate. We need a solution before the end of the meeting."

Instead of putting on pressure and pushing your group to do it *now*, move to step two and recreate. "Recreate" means to move away from the task. Go and do something else. Get a cup of coffee. Talk about another agenda item. Read a book. Tell jokes. Break for lunch. Let your subconscious mind go to work on the task.

To "oscillate" means to switch back and forth between focusing on the task and moving away from it. Some people call this procrastinating.

Most teams tend to stick to focusing. They push themselves to find a solution. Instead they often become stuck, as the creative juices dry up.

Creativity flows best when you are relaxed. When the pressure is off to come up with an immediate solution, the subconscious mind goes to work. Insights occur.

Try doing this with your next team task. Discuss the task, move away from it and then move back. You may need to do this several times in the course of the meeting. At no time should you pressure your team to come up with a creative solution NOW. Let the creative process occur naturally.

DON'T SHOW YOUR EMOTIONS

1. Do you feel that showing your emotions is a sign of weakness, especially in a business setting?

2. Do you try to hide your reactions when listening to other people?

3. Do you think that keeping emotions under strict control is the sign of a strong leader?

4. Do you feel uncomfortable when other people react emotionally?

An interesting study was conducted about how humans react to automated management. Two groups of people performed the same tasks. One group was led by a human supervisor, the other took its orders from a computer-generated program.

The group led by the human supervisor performed far above the other group. Why? Because human beings respond to human beings. What sets the human apart from the computer program? Emotions. Human beings respond to the emotions of another human being. If a supervisor is pleased, angry, frustrated, sympathetic, encouraging, demanding, enthusiastic or happy, his subordinates will react with similar emotions.

A team reacts in the same way to the team leader. If you keep your emotions tightly buttoned down, so will the rest of the team members. You'll never know how they really feel about what is happening. Your own lack of emotion will isolate you from your team members.

Showing emotions does not mean being out of control. It simply means responding to people in a human manner. If you are pleased with them, show it. If you are angry, be open about the anger. If you are enthusiastic, let others know. In the experiment mentioned earlier, one of the reasons why the workers failed to produce in response to the computer program is that they received no emotional feedback. All they had were numbers, statistics and work assignments. The computer never said, "That's a great idea!" or "You're doing well," or "Keep up the good work."

When you are open and human in your emotional response to your team members, you foster their creativity. It's hard for them to be creative if they expend all their energy on hiding their feelings.

Laughter opens the creative channels. So does enthusiasm. Even anger does. Sometimes you will find a creative solution to your problem because you are angry about it.

Nothing urges human beings to try harder than positive emotional feedback from other human beings. This same kind of feedback from you to your team members draws out their creativity and leads them to the third phase of empowerment: productivity.

SELF-EMPOWERMENT: FROM DON'TS TO DOS

FROM DON'T MAKE MISTAKES TO DO TAKE A RISK

Are you taking any risks in your life? You can answer that question by looking at your error rate. If you make few errors, you probably do things that are familiar and routine. However, if you try things that you have not tried before, or try new approaches, you will make your share of mistakes.

You may not feel comfortable with mistakes. Even the way you were graded in school was designed to tell you that correct answers were good and that incorrect answers were bad. Consider this chart of most school grading systems:

A = right more than 90 percent of the time
B = right more than 80 percent of the time
C = right more than 70 percent of the time
D = right more than 60 percent of the time
Less than 60 percent correct: YOU FAIL!

You soon learned that it was wrong to make a mistake. With this kind of attitude, you won't take many risks. Failing even a little penalizes you disproportionately to the rest of your success — being wrong just 15 percent of the time means a B average. No wonder you opt for the tried and true!

How can you strengthen your risk-taking ability? Make it a point to take at least one risk a week. Eat something you've never tried before. Do something outside your area of expertise. Invest in a new idea.

FROM DON'T WASTE TIME TO DO GO WITH THE FLOW

You may be one of those people who has a list that covers every moment of the day. Your day planner may be filled in meticulously, with every minute accounted for and each appointment carefully planned. You may be proud of your time-management ability and consider it one of your strengths. Yet, this same strength can be a weakness when it comes to dealing with your team.

When you look at each minute as being either useful or wasted, you are arbitrarily making a judgment. Standing in line at the bank may be a waste of time to you, yet to the person behind you, this may be a golden opportunity to think through a problem. Dealing with a flat tire may seem a terrible waste of time in a busy day, yet someone else may see it as an adventure outside the usual routine. It's all a matter of learning to "go with the flow."

You may find this a risky undertaking. It means giving up control of time when the circumstances warrant it. You may have to throw out your list, your agenda, your day book or your planner. But as we have seen earlier in this chapter, letting go of time allows people to tap into their creativity.

Try an experiment. For one day, do not use a list or look at your planner or — if you feel particularly bold — do not wear a watch. See what happens when you have a "timeless" day. At first you will feel insecure and anxious because you have learned to rely on external things like lists and clocks to maintain control. Try to relax and let the day happen to you. Get used to the feeling of timelessness. Trust in your own inner time piece and sense of space. Go with the flow.

FROM DON'T PROCRASTINATE TO DO PAUSE NOW AND THEN

The poet Doug King put it succinctly, "Learn to pause ... or nothing worthwhile will catch up with you." What problem are you working on right now that would benefit from a pause?

It could be something as simple as what to buy for a friend's birthday, or it could be something as complex as how to rewrite a computer program. You've probably been concentrating hard on the problem, worrying over it like an old dog with a bone. You may feel that you've come up against a brick wall, that your internal fountain of creativity has dried up or that your brain has turned to mush. You may even have a deadline hanging over you that makes you feel pressured into solving the problem quickly.

This is the moment to pause. Walk away from the problem. Do something else. Go and talk over baseball scores with the gang in the coffee room. Write a note to your cousin. Take a walk around the block. Think about last summer's vacation. Allow the muse of creativity to whisper in your ear. Get into the habit of pausing when looking for a solution to a problem.

FROM DON'T SHOW YOUR EMOTIONS TO DO EXPRESS FEELINGS

Some people see their emotions as allies and friends that connect them with life. They listen to what they are feeling and respond accordingly. For others, emotions are uncomfortable.

One of the reasons why you may not show emotion is that you may not know what emotion to show! Perhaps you are the intellectual type, so you're not sure how to connect with what you are feeling. Or perhaps you fear that if you communicate your feelings, you may lose control. Perhaps your emotions are locked up inside.

Make a list of every emotion you can think of. See how long a list you can generate. When you feel you can't think of any more emotions, go through the list and check off any emotions that you have experienced in the last month. Make a note of what happened to cause that emotion.

Then, look at the emotions you haven't checked off. Think about what kind of situation would cause you to experience those emotions. Now think about the following questions:

1. Have you checked off only "good" emotions? Or only "bad" emotions? What do you think happened to the others?

2. What kinds of situations elicit an emotional response from you? Do you see a pattern emerging?

3. Have you experienced some of the situations for the emotions you haven't checked off? What happened to the emotions in those situations?

4. Pick two positive emotions that you haven't checked off. Can you create a situation that will elicit those emotions?

Now write down some of the situations that you have experienced with your team. Put an appropriate emotional response next to each one. Did your team know how you felt in the situation? If not, jot down some ideas on how you could show this emotion in a constructive way.

Emotions are always tricky. You need to learn how to feel them, how to show them and how to use them. These two lists will give you some guidelines. Keep reminding yourself that your team needs your emotions in order to be able to free their own.

6

GETTING OUT OF COMFORT ZONES

Despite all your efforts, your team members still seem to get stuck easily. They go round and round in circles, accomplishing little and frustrating both you and themselves. What's going on?

You and your team may be stuck in a comfort zone. A comfort zone is a little like a rut. It's the way you always do things. It's made up of habits, norms, patterns of thinking and expectations. Once you get into a comfort zone, it's difficult to pull yourself out.

You've already come a long way from your own personal comfort zone in terms of how you now act as the team leader. To get things done, you're using your personal power rather than the comfort zone of positional power. You're allowing your team members to accept responsibility for a variety of tasks rather than remaining in the comfort zone of doing everything yourself. You're continually reminding yourself to move out of your old core beliefs, and you're leaving behind the limiting don'ts as you deal with your team.

Although you've made a lot of progress with your own personal comfort zone, your team still may be stuck in its comfort zone. It's up to you to help members break out and break free.

You start by determining what comfort zones they are in. Which ones are keeping them stuck?

THREE COMFORT ZONES THAT KILL CREATIVITY

"That's not the way we always do it!"

The way it's always been done is one of the most destructive comfort zones for a team. You can tell when your team has moved into this particular comfort zone by the phrases members use to respond to ideas. Listen for the following comments:

> "We tried that once. It didn't work."
> "We've never done it that way before."
> "The budget never will cover it."
> "It'll never be approved by management."
> "This doesn't fit within the regulations."
> "What about proper procedures?"
> "We must be practical about this."

You can hear the judgmental voices. These phrases are
a sure-fire way to kill creativity and, at the same time,
they put down the person who dared to think
creatively. These phrases also give team members a
way to avoid dealing with an idea that may not fit into
their comfort zones. No wonder the team becomes
stuck!

If you recognize this in your team, challenge the
members to substantiate the phrase. Treat the comfort-
zone phrase as a problem that needs a solution. For
example, if the comfort zone dictates that an idea
won't fit in the budget, how can the idea be modified
so that it does fit within the budget?

"That's not our job!"

This is another comfort zone that teams experience.
When a team sees itself as an isolated unit, it does not
consider its impact on the organization as a whole.
One of the reasons it is so important for your team to
see its place in the "big picture" is that it eliminates
any questions about what is or isn't the team's job.

Here's a story that illustrates what happens when a
team feels it is part of a much bigger picture.

A group of workers is digging a hole. When asked
what they are doing, they reply, "Digging a hole."
However, if that same group knows where its
particular task fits into the larger task, the workers
might have a different reply when asked what they are
doing. If they know that the hole they are digging will
provide a foundation for the pilings of a bridge, they
might say, "Building a bridge over this river."

If the hole is not deep enough, the uninformed group would say, "It's not our job to measure the depth of the hole." If the sides keep collapsing, the uninformed group would say, "It's not our job to worry about the sides of the hole."

But the informed group, knowing where its job fits into the overall scheme of things, will take responsibility for both the hole and its function in the finished bridge. As a result, these workers might take on tasks that are not necessarily part of "their job."

"This is good enough."

Why settle for excellent when good enough will do? Many organizations reward mediocrity. All they ask is that their employees meet a minimum standard to receive paychecks. There is no incentive to go beyond that standard. "Oh well, it's close enough" sums up this comfort zone.

Your team probably has learned what it needs to do to get by. Members have created a comfort zone that allows them to accept "good enough." Now, you need to destroy that comfort zone.

To do this, encourage your team to generate ideas. Usually when an idea is presented, someone decides that it is "good enough," and the group goes to work on the idea. However, if the group presents a number of ideas, there may be at least one that is better than good enough. It even may be excellent.

Insisting that the team produce several solutions to a problem can prevent settling for the first idea that comes up. You can lead your group through a brainstorming session if it seems stuck for new ideas.

Here's a brainstorming method that you can use.

Step One   Play the numbers game. See how many ideas your team members can generate. Encourage them to shout them out spontaneously without stopping for evaluation. Make sure that all team members withhold judgment on any idea. "No comment" is a sensible ground rule.

Step Two   Write the ideas down and number them. People respond to increasing numbers. If you caught six fish the last time you went fishing, you'll want to catch seven today. The same holds true for ideas. As your team sees the numbers increase, it will work harder to generate more ideas, thereby further increasing the numbers.

Step Three   Set a time limit. This forces your team members to push for as many ideas as they can generate. It also prevents them from spending time on personal evaluation before sharing an idea.

Step Four   Treat each idea equally. Do not
react to any idea that is generated,
even if you think it is foolish,
irrelevant, off-the-wall or brilliant. It
doesn't matter during the
brainstorming session. When your
team members see that ideas are
not evaluated instantly, they will
feel free to offer more creative
ideas.

Once you have a wealth of ideas, you can begin the
evaluation process. Remind your team that you are
looking for ideas that are beyond "good enough."
Challenge team members to achieve excellence. Go
for the gold!

Whenever you suspect that your team is just spinning
its wheels, look for a comfort zone. Sometimes it will
be your comfort zone that is holding the team back.
Have you slipped unconsciously into the authoritarian
management style? Are you taking on all the
responsibility? Are you pushing the team to come up
with a quick solution?

Sometimes the team will create new comfort zones
that are just as unproductive as the ones you have
worked to overcome. Each time, you need to evaluate
what is happening and counteract any existing comfort
zones.

GETTING OUT OF YOUR LEADERSHIP COMFORT ZONE

Remember your reaction when your boss appointed you leader of the new team? After you got over the excitement of being chosen to do the job, what were your next thoughts? "Oh, no! How can I run a group like that? Frank will be difficult as usual, and no doubt Mona will be miffed that she didn't get the job. It won't take them long to figure out that I'm new at this leadership business. It'll probably be one long battle for control and power. George will challenge everything I say — he always does. And Grace? She's probably the only one I can count on to support me."

This was the beginning of your comfort zone as a leader. Then, you probably went further.

"Boy, I'm really dreading this. I'm no good at getting people to do things, even if my boss does think I'm the best person for the job. I'll probably mess up the whole thing. I hate having to run the meetings. I'll have to watch every little thing I say and do."

Now you've created a comfort zone. It doesn't sound comfortable, but it's what you have instructed your subconscious to create so things work out just the way you planned them! Your comfort zone paves the way for a difficult team and a hesitant leadership style.

When you get what you ordered — remember that first meeting — you actually congratulate your subconscious on doing such a good job. You even tell it to keep up the good work. "Well, it's just what I expected. Everyone but Grace is difficult to work with, and I really made some stupid mistakes in the way I handled the rest of the team."

Comfort zones give people an excuse not to do anything. The comfort zones that your team uses to excuse its inaction are no different from the comfort zones that you create. Obviously, if your team is made up of difficult people, there's not much you can do about them. If you are unexperienced, no one will expect you to do any more than the bare minimum. You can begin to see why these are called comfort zones.

If you decide that you don't like the comfort zone, you always can break free from it. Here's how:

1. Make sure that what you are experiencing is a comfort zone. Check that you did, in fact, set it up for yourself.

2. What is it that you can avoid doing because of this comfort zone?

3. Will you feel uncomfortable if you have to do these activities? (If the answer is "yes," good! This means you'll be forced outside your comfort zone.)

4. What kind of situation will force you to do these activities? Set that situation up in your mind. Picture it clearly. Picture yourself doing the activities. Tell your subconscious that this is what you really want.

5. Remind yourself that you won't feel comfortable in this new situation. Otherwise, you'll quickly fall back on the old comfort zone.

When you think of leading your team, picture yourself dealing with each of the team members in a positive, effective way. Picture yourself learning new leadership techniques and trying them out. Be prepared for the trial-and-error process, especially the errors you will encounter as you learn.

Allow yourself to move from an old comfort zone to a new uncomfortable place where self-empowerment can begin.

7

WHY YOUR TEAM GETS "STUCK"

At this point, your team should exhibit the characteristics of an empowered team. Members are building, developing and increasing their power through cooperation, sharing and working together. They are committed to common goals, taking risks and demonstrating initiative and creativity.

Perhaps your team seems to be empowered only part of the time. Although the team members are no longer stuck in their comfort zones, there are still times when you feel that you're back in that first meeting. What is going on?

There are three possibilities:

1. The team is being controlled by its norms.

2. The team is being controlled by your unfounded assumptions.

3. The team is being controlled by the rules.

NORMS

In addition to common comfort zones that cause inaction in a team, the team itself can create comfort zones based on its past experiences and its beliefs. These comfort zones are called "norms." Unlike the comfort zones you have been dealing with, norms can affect a group positively as well as negatively. Some norms energize a team; some sap the team.

How do you recognize a norm in action? First of all, a group's norm is the same as an individual's habit. It's made up of three components:

1. What is important (values)

2. What is seen to be true (beliefs)

3. How it is supposed to be done (behavior)

You use norms every day. For example, when you visit a library, the norm is to speak softly. You wouldn't dream of shouting a question to a colleague across the room. When you get on the bus, the norm is to resist moving to the rear as more people get on. If that weren't a norm, the bus driver wouldn't continually have to urge people to move back!

What's the norm for elevator behavior? Face the front and don't talk to anyone you don't know. For express lines in the supermarket? Count the items in your basket and those in the basket of the person in front of you!

Some norms change so rapidly that you may not be sure what they are. The norms of dating are hard to keep up with, for example. At one time, the man called, made the date and paid all expenses. Is that the norm today, or has it changed?

Some norms go outside established rules. The law limits your speed on expressways, but the norm usually is to go five to 10 miles over that limit.

Norms are both changeable and fixed, rational and irrational. They create your behaviors and guide your life. They are far beyond comfort zones, and yet they can become comfort zones.

Think about the norms in your organization.

- What is the stated starting time? What time do people really start working? The latter is the norm for starting the job.

- How long is coffee break? How long do people actually take? The latter is your company's norm for coffee breaks.

- When is the month-end report due? When is it usually sent out? You know the norm for the month-end report.

- Who is invited to the Christmas party? Who usually goes? The norm may not be the same as the invitation list.

- What is the policy for equal opportunity? How does it actually work? The norm may not measure up to the policy.

- Is there a dress code? How do people really dress? The norm may set a code, even if it's not written down.

In some cases, even though a policy may be in place, the norm does not conform to it. In others, no policy exists, yet the norm creates an unwritten policy.

Your team is affected by the norms it has chosen to use in the team setting. The team norms create its culture and policies.

WHAT IS IMPORTANT?

Think about the norms for your team. Start with the norms that encompass the values, or what is important to the team. Remember that norms can have both a positive and a negative effect on the team's behavior. Ask yourself this question:

What does my team consider important?

- the weekly paycheck?
- the progress it has made?
- reaching the targeted goals?
- learning from other members?
- getting through the meeting?
- not rocking the boat?
- doing what management wants?
- setting an example of teamwork?

The possibilities are endless. As you can see, what is important to the team will affect the team's behavior. For example, if it is important not to rock the boat, no one is going to do anything outside the boundaries set by management.

One way to help your team members recognize their "important" norms is to ask each person to make a list of what he thinks is important. Discuss these lists and determine which norms positively affect team performance and which should be discarded. Remember to get consensus on what is important to the team.

WHAT IS SEEN TO BE TRUE?

What you see as being true creates your beliefs. If you believe that you are an excellent dancer, then that is how you see yourself. However, it may or may not be true!

Your team also has beliefs about itself and about its members. Listen carefully for the clues to these beliefs. If you hear phrases like the following, then you know that a belief is being stated.

> "We're not really equipped to deal with that."
>
> "There's only one way to handle this."
>
> "No matter what we do, it won't make any difference."
>
> "Management doesn't take any notice of our reports."
>
> "This team idea is just a fad."
>
> "All this work is a waste of time and effort."
>
> "Why bother? We don't have the authority to enforce this."

Some of these statements may have an element of truth in them, but that element of truth now is seen as the absolute truth. The belief is formed. These are all negative belief statements.

When you hear a negative belief statement, challenge your team to provide the basis for it. In other words, look for the truth. If the group says, "Why bother? We don't have the authority to enforce this," discuss what kind of authority is needed. Who has this authority? How can you use that person's authority? Encourage your team to go beyond the negative belief and turn it into a positive action.

Fortunately, there are also positive belief statements. Listen for them and point them out to your team.

Encourage the team to act upon these statements and treat them as truths. Here are some positive belief statements.

"We can make a difference to the project."
"I know we can learn those new procedures."
"We're lucky to be on this team."
"Management is really listening to us."
"We'll find the resources we need."

As team leader, you need to use your listening skills to determine what your team sees as truth. Become an expert in negative belief busting!

HOW IT IS SUPPOSED TO BE DONE

A woman was renowned for her baked ham recipe. One day a reporter from a cooking magazine came to her house to watch her prepare the ham. The woman took out the large ham, cut it into two portions and placed them side by side in the pan. The reporter asked her why she cut the ham in two pieces. "That's part of the recipe," said the woman. "That's the way it is supposed to be prepared. It's the way my mother always did it." The reporter wasn't content with this answer, so he visited the woman's mother. "Oh," she said, "My mother taught me to do it that way." Fortunately, her mother was still alive. The reporter visited her in the nursing home and asked her the same question. "Why," said the woman, "I never had a pan big enough to hold a whole ham, so I had to cut it in two."

Your team members operate on the same principle! They may do things in a certain way because they think "that is the way it is supposed to be done."

Do your remember the discomfort you felt at being the leader when you had your first meeting with the team? Why? Because you and your team acted *the way you were supposed to act*. You told them what to do, and they did it.

It has taken you quite a while to move beyond that norm and begin to create your empowered team. Some norms based on how things are supposed to be done still may linger and prevent your team from catching fire. For example, someone on your team may have a higher organizational status than the others. Do you unconsciously defer to that person's wishes and ideas? *That's the way it is supposed to be done.* But does it help the team members feel equal and appreciated?

Do you always hold your team meetings in the boardroom? *That is the way it is supposed to be done.* What would happen if you changed the norm and held the meetings over coffee in the cafeteria?

Do you always appoint one person to take minutes? *That is the way it is supposed to be done.* What would happen if everyone kept his own version of the minutes and then circulated them to the other members?

Once you begin to examine the norms of yourself and your team, it becomes an exciting exercise in what to keep and what to discard. You and your team should work together to create the culture that you want. Choosing and using norms in this way empowers your team to have control over its actions and behaviors.

UNFOUNDED ASSUMPTIONS

There is yet another norm to consider: "You get what you expect." As a team leader, you have particular expectations for your team. You could call these "assumptions." You assume that the team members will respond in a certain way. The problem with assumptions is that they often become self-fulfilling prophecies.

For example, if you assume that you will have difficulty with a certain team member when you discuss the budget, you might preface your remarks by saying, "You probably won't agree with them, Mary, but I have the figures for our fiscal projections." Your assumption is played out in your words. You have just given Mary permission to disagree with you, and she'll gladly meet your expectation. After the meeting, you'll say to yourself. "Just as I expected. Mary gave me a hard time on the budget."

Or, you may assume that everyone understands the task at hand. Before you begin to outline the task, you might say, "There shouldn't be any questions on this..." And there aren't. But this unfounded assumption may result in a botched project because one team member didn't feel comfortable asking a question when you assumed that he already had all the information.

You'll hear your unfounded assumptions over and over again.

> "This won't make you happy, Jerry..."
> "This should only take a couple of minutes..."
> "This is pretty simple stuff..."
> "I don't need to go into the whys of this..."
> "I guess George will want to respond to this..."
> "This may upset some of you..."

You, in essence, force your team to fulfill your prophecies, sometimes to the detriment of your team's productivity or creativity.

FOLLOW THE RULES

There is a lot of pressure in our culture to follow the rules. We are taught that the sky is blue, the grass is green and cows are never purple. Those are the rules. If you challenge the rules, you must be a troublemaker.

Alexander the Great was a troublemaker. The rules said that if someone could untie the Gordian knot, he would become ruler of Asia. The Gordian knot consisted of miles of ropes tied and retied into a shapeless mass. Alexander realized that the knot was immensely complicated and could not be untied. So Alexander broke the rules. He sliced the knot in half with his sword, and Asia was his.

Sometimes the rules you blindly follow lost their relevance a long time ago. For example, look at the letters on a typewriter or computer keyboard. They have no pattern, no rhythm. Remember how hard it was to make your fingers follow this nonsensical alphabet? But the rules say that is the way keyboards are configured. Why? Because when the first typewriters were built, the manufacturer received complaints that typists went too quickly and jammed the keys. The keyboard was redesigned to slow down the typists.

Today, keyboards still are manufactured using the same configuration. The rules say you must learn that Q W E R T Y U I O P are in the top row. No one ever has challenged this rule.

Look at the rules that govern your team. Are some of them obsolete? What would happen if you broke some of the rules? Ask why. Or why not. Have a rule-bashing session. Find out what rules really bug your team members. Can you get rid of those rules? Change them? Revise them?

Be innovative. Color the cow purple if it makes your team work more creatively and productively!

Free your team by using its norms to create future actions, by removing your own unfounded assumptions and by changing the rules. These are surefire ways to get your team "unstuck!"

SELF-EMPOWERMENT AND YOUR NORMS

You can become just as stuck as your team members. If you experience internal conflict as you work in new ways with your team members, it may signal that you are infringing upon your internal values and beliefs. You may have learned the most effective behaviors, but they do not support the things that are most important to you. If you achieve your goals but still feel vaguely unsatisfied, you may be experiencing incongruity between your norms and your actions. That is, your actions do not support your beliefs. To be effective, you need to achieve congruency, a state in which everything you do supports everything you believe. To succeed as a leader, you need to be consciously aware of what you consider to be important, how you measure success and failure and what internal rules guide your behavior.

Like all human beings, you work from an internal hierarchy of values. These values determine what you consider to be right, wrong, good, bad or important. These values come from your past, from your family and friends. They come from your present, from your environment and social sphere. These values change as you continue through life.

If your actions support your values, you will feel whole and fulfilled. If not, you become stuck! For example, if you have worked hard to achieve a certain financial status, but one of your values is that money is the root of all evil, you are not going to feel comfortable with your new-found wealth. In the same way, your values about adequacy also will change. The car you once drove no longer seems luxurious enough, so you'll now move up to the larger, more expensive model.

It's important to recognize your current values and how they affect your role as leader. You can do this by asking the "what's important?" question. Ask yourself, "What's important to me about working?", to which you might answer, "learning new things." Then ask, "What's important about learning new things?", to which you might respond, "using my creativity." Then, "What's important about your creativity?" Continue to ask and answer questions in this manner until you are satisfied that you have a list of your values about learning new things. Then go back and ask the primary question again, "What's important to me about working?"

You have a list of your values about work. Go one step further. Discover your hierarchy, that is, what's most important and what's least important on your list. One way to do this is to rank all the items on your list. If you find this difficult, try comparing the items. Take the first one and compare it to the rest. Which is the most important? Do this with each item until you have created a comparative ranking.

Now you have your hierarchy of values about work.

The next step is to discover what will satisfy your primary values. Let's suppose that your primary value was "getting the job done right." Now ask yourself, "What situation would make me feel that I got the job done right?" "What causes me to experience this value?" Be as specific as possible as you create the scenarios and behaviors that will support this value. Do this with the top four values on your hierarchy.

Compare your scenarios and behaviors with your actual experiences as team leader. Perhaps your leadership role is in direct conflict with your values!

Most people will experience some conflict. But if you recognize where the conflict originates, you can cope with it positively. Work with your values, remembering that they can be changed, or work with your behavior, changing it to support the value. Be flexible in your approach.

Instead of feeling uneasy about your leadership role, try to understand what's going on inside you and begin to generate new behaviors.

8

MOVING FROM DEPENDENCE TO SELF-RELIANCE

The time has come to move your team on to a new level of interaction. You are going to create an empowered, self-reliant, interdependent team! This almost sounds contradictory, but it's important in order for your team to perform at its best.

First, you must help your team members become dependent on each other. You've already started this process. Let's look at the dependence dynamic that has developed in your team.

DEPENDENCE

When you called the first team meeting, you brought together a group of people who were dependent on you as their leader. They depended on you to tell them what to do, to make sure they did it and to let them know if they weren't doing it.

The authoritarian style of management fosters dependence on the manager or leader. Unfortunately, dependence does not empower a team. If anything, it saps the power from a team and leaves it helpless if a leader is not in place.

As a result, in the dependent setting, if you didn't show up on time for a meeting, your team members would sit around and wait for you. No one would even consider starting the meeting without you. Similarly, in the dependent setting, no one volunteered to do a task. Everybody waited to be told which tasks to do.

As you quickly found out, the dependent team is low in energy and enthusiasm.

INDEPENDENCE

So, you started to foster independence. You encouraged each team member to be responsible for his own tasks. You expected each person to contribute to the smooth operation of the team. You allowed your team members to set their own standards and create their own guidelines. If you remember the first analogy of empowerment — building your own house — you empowered each team member to complete his own part of the house.

INTERDEPENDENCE

Now, you want to build a house *together.* That is the essence of teamwork. The time has come to create an interdependent team, a team that recognizes and uses each member's strengths to compensate for each member's weaknesses.

To begin this interdependent process, work with your team to identify its strengths and weaknesses. Ask each member to answer the following questions individually.

1. What were your most enjoyable work experiences? What made them enjoyable? What skills or abilities did you use?

2. How did you interact with people in these work experiences? Were you a coach, a coordinator, a director, an individualist, a manager, a team leader or a team member?

3. What kind of results did you achieve from these work experiences?

You can ask the same questions about experiences outside of the work environment.

Now you have a pretty good idea of the strengths of your team members. You know their individual abilities, their subject matter expertise, the way they like to interact with others and the kinds of results they usually attain.

It is a lot easier to pinpoint weaknesses. As you discuss one team member's strengths, ask the others to indicate areas of weakness. Sometimes it's a good idea to use a chart so that everyone sees the patterns of the team.

Building a house with an interdependent team means that the plumbers do the plumbing, the electricians do the wiring and the carpenters do the framework. In other words, each member contributes his own expertise to create the finished house.

An interdependent team recognizes, acknowledges and respects the strengths of its members. Members of an interdependent team feel good about themselves and their contributions to the team. They do not compete. In fact, they move beyond cooperation to collaboration.

SELF-RELIANCE

Once you have encouraged your team to move from dependence to independence to interdependence, it's time to deal with the issue of self-reliance again.

The team must be self-reliant to be fully empowered. Self-reliance is a balance between counterdependence and overdependence.

THE COUNTERDEPENDENT TEAM

The counterdependent team has several characteristics.

- It works autonomously, never interacting with other teams, departments or divisions.

- It believes that no one else or no other team can perform the tasks as well as it does.

- It is frequently suspicious of the motives of other departments or of management.

- It never consults other teams, departments or divisions before making a decision or implementing a change.

The counterdependent team strives for too much independence from the rest of the organization. It sees itself as a "lone wolf" who must protect its interests at all cost. It has no trust in any other area of the organization.

THE OVERDEPENDENT TEAM

The overdependent team is unable to act as a true team. Its characteristics are as follows:

- It often makes decisions based on avoiding conflict with any other group, person or department, rather than on what's best for the situation.

- It depends too much on other teams, departments or divisions to carry out the team tasks.

- It requires frequent feedback from management and refuses to move forward without such feedback.

- It overconsults with others, bringing in so much information that it suffers from "paralysis of analysis," the inability to make a decision.

THE SELF-RELIANT TEAM

The self-reliant team strikes a balance between these two extremes.

On one hand, it is able to take responsibility for its own well-being and purpose. The team is self-empowered. On the other hand, when help is needed, the self-reliant team will seek out expertise and assistance from other teams, departments or divisions.

The self-reliant, interdependent team is a truly empowered team!

SELF-EMPOWERMENT AND SELF-RELIANCE

Are you self-reliant? Do you allow others to help you? Do you take responsibility for your own well-being when necessary?

Self-reliance is a balance between allowing others to help when necessary and taking responsibility for your own well-being. Examine specific situations. When do you feel you don't need anyone? In which situations do you tend to be overdependent, that is, needing other people to make you feel OK? You may discover that you behave one way at home and another at work. Or, you may act one way with your boss and another with your team.

Finding the balance between allowing others to help and being personally responsible is particularly important for the leader of a self-directed team. To achieve this balance, you need to ask yourself, "When do I need the support of the team?" and "When do I need to take the responsibility myself?" For example, you may need your team to work through a particular project because some members have expertise in this area that you do not have. But, it may be your responsibility to take this project to upper management — that is something the team cannot do for you.

Problems arise when you lose this balance. For example, you may decide that you have to oversee every little detail of the project, even though you do not have the expertise. Or you may want to bring along several team members to "back you up" when you talk to your boss. In the first case, your team members will resent your intrusion. In the second, they may feel that you are too insecure to deal with the boss by yourself.

Whenever you feel yourself moving to counter-dependence ("I don't need them") or to over-dependence ("I don't want to do this myself"), it's time to pause and bring balance to the situation.

9

THE FUEL THAT KEEPS EMPOWERMENT GOING

You now have an empowered team.

- It is enabled, committed and productive.
- It moves easily outside of its comfort zones.
- It chooses norms that create a positive culture.
- It is self-reliant and interdependent.

How do you keep it that way? How do you keep the fires of empowerment burning? Better still, how do you ensure that empowerment fuels itself? In other words, now that you've got your team turned on, how can you make sure it doesn't turn off when you're not looking?

Your team members will do that for you. If you provide an environment in which their basic needs are met, they will continue to do their work without prompting from you.

What are the basic needs of human beings? According to Dr. William Glasser, four inherent needs must be met for humans to be satisfied:

1. The need to belong

2. The need for power

3. The need for freedom

4. The need for fun

Are you meeting all these needs for your team members?

THE NEED TO BELONG

People will go to great lengths to belong. Some join clubs, some collect stamps, some have pets, some have families, some play tennis, some play golf and some play the saxophone. Most people fulfill their primary needs to belong, to love, to share and to cooperate within their family circles. Others meet this need in their professional lives. A functioning, empowered team meets this need to belong, too.

Within the team, a team member can:

- feel important, needed, understood, supported and appreciated
- experience acceptance and respect
- benefit from shared ideas, cooperation and joint efforts
- enjoy camaraderie, fellowship and togetherness

These all meet team members' need to belong.

THE NEED FOR POWER

Everyone needs to feel that, at some point in life, he has power over the moment. Power comes in many forms. It can be the positional power of a manager, the traditional power of a parent or the influential power of a politician. Power can mean as much as controlling the largest corporation in North America and as little as teaching a dog a new trick. Human beings have a need to experience power, in whatever form.

By its nature, the empowered team answers this need in its members.

Team members experience power when they:

- set a direction that is theirs to follow
- create policies that will affect the entire organization
- make changes that have a real and lasting effect
- teach others
- empower each other

Each member of the empowered team feels personally powerful and able to work to the fullest of his potential, using the strengths, abilities and skills that are recognized by the rest of the team.

THE NEED FOR FREEDOM

The need for freedom is probably the strongest of the basic human needs. Battles have been fought, countries have been divided, worlds have been discovered and lives have been lost — all in the name of freedom. Saying that team members can find freedom within the team almost seems a contradiction of terms because freedom usually implies an individual's right. Yet, in an empowered team, team members enjoy a great deal of freedom because they can:

- take responsibility for the success or failure of the team
- choose and generate tasks
- learn new skills from each other
- trust each other to provide support and cooperation

Unlike some teams that are run in an authoritative manner, your participative team embodies personal freedom.

In many groups, the three inherent basic needs — the need to belong, the need for power and the need for freedom — often are at odds with each other.

- How often have you been involved in a group where you felt you really didn't fit in, and the group made no effort to make you feel comfortable? Your need to belong was not met.

- How often have you been in a group that specialized in "power plays," with each member trying to be in control? Your need for power was not met.

- How often have you been in a group in which your job was to do what you were told, no questions asked? Your need for freedom was not met.

One of the easiest ways to recognize a truly empowered team is to consider how well the needs of its members are being met.

THE NEED FOR FUN

What about the need for fun? Somehow that doesn't seem relevant in a business situation. Surely that need is met somewhere else, like the bowling team or coffee break or in aerobic dance classes. Unfortunately, because of these assumptions, the need for fun is rarely met in day-to-day work relationships.

Yet, this need is important, not frivolous. It is the only need that is completely human. Laughter is unique to the human species. No other creatures have the need for fun. So what makes it so important to you and your team?

Think back to the meeting for which you first planned a celebratory event. Remember, you brought in doughnuts. It didn't seem like much at the time, but remember what happened at that meeting? Your team members relaxed, made jokes, enjoyed the treat and laughed a lot. The rest of the meeting seemed to just fly by. Everyone was in a mellow, cooperative mood. It was the first time that you got a taste of what it was like to lead an empowered team. All as the result of a box of doughnuts?

Well, not quite. The doughnuts started a chain reaction. Because you set up the circumstances for relaxing and having fun, your team members did just that. There was a lot of laughter, and a lot of camaraderie and kidding around. But more importantly, that was the meeting when a lot of work got done, many decisions were made and some creative ideas took flight.

When humans laugh, two things happen:

1. They learn easier.

2. They heal faster.

An experiment was conducted on a group of third-grade school children. Half of the class was taught a history subject by an excellent teacher who used classic teaching methods. The other half was taught the same subject by a teacher dressed as a clown who made the children laugh. At the end of the teaching period, both groups were tested.

The children in the group that had laughed as they learned scored significantly higher in knowledge than the group who had been taught in the traditional manner.

When you laugh, you release your creativity and turn on the learning mechanisms in your brain. You'll make better decisions, take more exciting risks and cooperate more with others when you have fun.

Something else happens in your brain when you laugh. Laughter triggers the release of endorphins into the bloodstream. These are the natural pain killers of your body. Have you ever noticed that you forget your aches and pains when you enjoy yourself?

In a study in a large Canadian hospital, cancer patients were divided into two groups. One group was treated in the usual manner, the other spent an hour a day in the "laugh room," a room filled with videotapes, cartoons, films, joke books and pictures. At the end of six months, the patients who laughed for an hour each day needed less pain medication than the patients who did not visit the "laugh room."

Remember, your team feels better and functions better when it laughs!

BEYOND EMPOWERMENT

The fuel that keeps a team empowered is simply meeting the inherent needs of the team. As long as team members' needs are met, the result will continue to be an empowered team. It is a self-fueling process.

Once you start empowerment, it will continue to run on the energy generated by the team.

SELF-EMPOWERING YOUR RIGHT BRAIN

If you looked at your brain, you would see that it is clearly divided into two portions: a right hemisphere and a left hemisphere. Each side of the brain is used for different types of thinking.

LEFT HEMISPHERE: logical, sequential, intellectual, verbal, analytical and linear

RIGHT HEMISPHERE: creative, emotional, lateral, imaginative, intuitive and fantastic

The way that most of us have been educated and trained encourages the use of our left-brain functions. As a result, you probably try to solve your problems with a logical, orderly approach.

The right brain, on the other hand, is the site of play, fun, humor and fantasy. As you learned earlier in this chapter, humor releases our creativity and heals our bodies. To access the positive properties of humor, therefore, you need to access your right brain.

Try this exercise.

1. Imagine a huge castle. Put it on top of a mountain. Imagine a fierce storm raging around the castle.

2. Now, slowly count to 10 in your head.

3. Now, answer this question: What color is the letter S? If you have difficulty with the question, keep pushing your brain to give the letter S a color.

You probably felt jarred by the last question. Your brain didn't seem able to handle it. You may not have been able to give a color to the letter S. Here's why.

When you pictured the castle and the storm, you performed a right brain function — you imagined something that probably didn't exist in your experience.

Then when you counted to 10 in your head, you performed a left-brain function — you remembered a sequential series of numbers.

When you were asked to give the letter S a color, you were still in your left brain, the logical side, and your left brain tried to answer the question logically. Of course, there is no logical answer, and so you felt dislocated and uncomfortable. If you continued to push for an answer, eventually you returned to your brain's right hemisphere, where you could imagine a letter S and give it a color.

Notice how easily you moved from your right brain (castle) to left brain (counting). But the move from left brain (counting) to right brain (letter S) was probably difficult. Studies have shown this to be true for most people. Because you were trained to use your left brain to solve problems, it is the area where you feel most comfortable. The right brain usually is left to its own devices!

Since play, fun, humor and fantasy occur in the right hemisphere, to enjoy them, therefore, you must move into that hemisphere.

People who think that play is frivolous, that if you're just playing at something you're not really working at it, or who think that work and play are mutually exclusive, probably are those who have the most difficulty moving from their left to their right brain. When you hear people say, "Stop playing games and get down to business," for example, they're probably stuck in their left-brain thinking patterns.

If the need to have fun is one of the most basic needs of all human beings, then the need to move into the right brain is also basic. How can you learn to move easily into your right brain and allow yourself to access the creativity and imagination that are there? One of the best ways is to force yourself to see things in a different light. For example, looking at the letter S in terms of color rather than in terms of sound, place in the alphabet, or shape forced you into a right-brain function. Jokes do this well. For example, what do Alexander the Great and Winnie the Pooh have in common? (They both have the same middle name.)

Usually you would try to classify Alexander the Great and Winnie the Pooh according to left-brain principles: who they were, what they did, and where they went. You would be hard pressed to find any similarities. But when you look at the joke from a different perspective, the answer is clear. If you can imagine this unlikely pair in the same context, you can put any two things together and find similarities: Dolls and three-hole punches, balloons and computers, magazines and frying pans. If you think hard enough, you'll find some kind of connection. This type of thinking is at the core of creativity.

There is a close relationship between the "ha ha" of humor and the "ah hah" of creativity.

Try this exercise to access your creative, humorous and fun right brain. Sit quietly and think of a problem that you have been concerned about. Imagine it as a formless shape on the table in front of you. What does it look like? What does it feel like? If it had a handle, what would it be like? Does the handle represent a clue to the solution of the problem?

Now, what would it be like if you...

- reversed it?
- turned it upside down?
- flattened it?
- chopped it up?
- rearranged it?
- stretched it?
- took it apart?
- turned it around?

Now, what does it have in common with...

- a shoe?
- a book?
- a picture?
- a carrot?
- a cup of coffee?

Look around the room and find objects for comparison. Your problem probably looks a lot different than when you started out! You can have fun with the problem, change it, rearrange it and solve it.

To meet your need to have fun, you continually must empower yourself to move from the logical to the irrational, from the verbal to the visual, from the intellectual to the emotional. Try it. You'll have fun in the process!

10

PUTTING IT ALL TOGETHER

Can you do it? Can you use the information you've learned from this handbook and put it all together to empower your self-directed team? Better still, can you use the information to empower yourself to become the leader of that team? How do you feel about implementing the ideas you've learned? Scared? Excited? Motivated? Intimidated?

These are all valid questions to consider as you begin to move from learning to doing. It's easy to read about how to do certain things. It's much harder to do them. So, how do you begin to do what you've been reading about?

Although you may think that certain chapters of this handbook have been more relevant to your particular situation while others really don't concern you, it still is best to start at the beginning.

Pull out a fresh sheet of paper and start to create a plan that you and your team can follow. Make two columns: one headed "Me" and the other "My Team." As you've seen throughout this handbook, empowering your team means first empowering yourself. Whatever needs to be done with the team, also must be done for you. Now put these two action plans side by side so that you can see their synergy.

Your first step is examining core beliefs. Review the core beliefs from Chapter Two. Jot them down in the column labeled "My Team" and add a note or two about how you see them affecting your behavior with your team. In the "Me" column, think about some of the inner-voice messages that your negative core beliefs carry. Work with one or two of them to change the belief at level one — the super-conscious.

Now think about participative management. You'll find those notes in Chapter Three. Under "My Team," write down the actions you plan to take with your team members to ensure that they benefit from your participative management style. Under "Me," review the plan you made for improving your management style and jot down some definite action steps you can take.

Let's move into the commitment area. In the "My Team" column, write out the direction your team has chosen. Do the same for yourself in the "Me" column. Now write out the goals, the resources and the support that your team has. Again, do the same for yourself. Write down two specific actions that you can take to celebrate and recognize first your team and then yourself.

Both you and your team need to be creative. Remember the four "don'ts" that limit creativity. Don't make mistakes. Don't waste time. Don't procrastinate. Don't show your emotions. Think about each "don't" and then brainstorm some ideas about how you can move from limits to liberation. Jot these ideas down for yourself and your team.

How good are you at recognizing comfort zones? Check back in Chapter Six for some guidelines on how to tell if your team is stuck in a comfort zone. Then, under "My Team," record some ways you can jolt members out of their comfort zones. Under "Me," draw a new picture of how you want to handle your leadership responsibilities.

Your team has norms that determine its behavior. Write down the norms that lead to more productive activity. Make some new positive assumptions about the team members. Rewrite the rules for your team. On your side of the sheet, jot down your values that are supported by your team experiences. Define and redefine these values until you feel that they are completely congruent with your team experiences.

Now look at the issue of self-reliance. In the "My Team" column, list everything that the team is solely responsible for. Then list everything that it needs support from others to do. Do the same thing for your column. What are you solely responsible for? When do you need the support of your team?

Finally, do a check to make sure that the needs of your individual team members are being met. In the "My Team" column, list the ways you can meet their needs for belonging, power, freedom and fun. In the "Me" column, list the ways your own needs are met.

Finish your plan of action by having fun! Try this right-brain exercise. Write down the name of one of your team members. Now, picture him clearly in your mind. Once you have a clear picture, try the same exercise that you did with your problem in Chapter Nine. Be silly. Reverse, turn upside down, stretch, flatten, blow up, shrink, change colors, size and shape. Make comparisons. What does this person have in common with...? Look around the room for inspiration. Enjoy the freedom of your right-brain manipulations. When you've run out of ideas for change and comparison, begin to jot down as many words as possible to describe this person's strengths and how he contributes to the team's success. Your right brain will give you a whole new picture of that team member. Do the same with each member of your team.

Now you have a complete plan of action. You have put it all together in a way that allows you to work on your own empowerment as well as the empowerment of your team.

What remains? To do it. To begin. To start work on your plan and carry out the actions you have written down. You now have the tools, the information and the knowledge to become an effective leader of a self-empowered team. Good luck!

Index

W

Buy two, get one free!

Each of our handbook series (LIFESTYLE, COMMUNICATION, PRODUCTIVITY, and LEADERSHIP) was designed to give you the most comprehensive collection of hands-on desktop references related to a specific topic. These handbooks are a great value at the regular price of $12.95 ($14.95 in Canada); plus, at the unbeatable offer of buy two at the regular price and get one free, you can't find a better value in learning resources. **To order**, see the back of this page for the entire handbook selection.

1. Fill out and send the entire page by mail to:

    National Press Publications
    6901 West 63rd Street
    P.O. Box 2949
    Shawnee Mission, Kansas 66201-1349

2. Or **FAX 1-913-432-0824**

3. Or call toll-free **1-800-258-7248** (**1-800-685-4142** in Canada)

Fill out completely:

Name _____

Organization _____

Address _____

City _____

State/Province _____ ZIP/Postal Code _____

Telephone (   ) _____

Method of Payment:

❏ Enclosed is my check or money order

❏ Please charge to:

    ❏ MasterCard   ❏ VISA   ❏ American Express

Signature _____ Exp. Date _____

Credit Card Number

❏ ❏ ❏ ❏ ❏ ❏ ❏ ❏ ❏ ❏ ❏ ❏ ❏ ❏

To order multiple copies for co-workers and friends: U.S. Can.

    20-50 copies..$8.50 $10.95

    More than 50 copies..$7.50 $ 9.95

VIP# 705-008422-093

OTHER DESKTOP HANDBOOKS

	Qty	Item#	Title	U.S.	Can.	Total
LEADERSHIP		410	The Supervisor's Handbook	$12.95	$14.95	
		418	Total Quality Management	$12.95	$14.95	
		421	Change: Coping with Tomorrow Today	$12.95	$14.95	
		459	Techniques of Successful Delegation	$12.95	$14.95	
		463	Powerful Leadership Skills for Women	$12.95	$14.95	
		494	Team-Building	$12.95	$14.95	
		495	How to Manage Conflict	$12.95	$14.95	
		469	Peak Performance	$12.95	$14.95	
COMMUNICATION		413	Dynamic Communication Skills for Women	$12.95	$14.95	
		414	The Write Stuff: *A Style Manual for Effective Business Writing*	$12.95	$14.95	
		417	Listen Up: *Hear What's Really Being Said*	$12.95	$14.95	
		442	Assertiveness: *Get What You Want Without Being Pushy*	$12.95	$14.95	
		460	Techniques to Improve Your Writing Skills	$12.95	$14.95	
		461	Powerful Presentation Skills	$12.95	$14.95	
		482	Techniques of Effective Telephone Communication	$12.95	$14.95	
		485	Personal Negotiating Skills	$12.95	$14.95	
		488	Customer Service: *The Key to Winning Lifetime Customers*	$12.95	$14.95	
		498	How to Manage Your Boss	$12.95	$14.95	
PRODUCTIVITY		411	Getting Things Done: *An Achiever's Guide to Time Management*	$12.95	$14.95	
		443	A New Attitude	$12.95	$14.95	
		468	Understanding the Bottom Line: *Finance for the Non-Financial Manager*	$12.95	$14.95	
		483	Successful Sales Strategies: *A Woman's Perspective*	$12.95	$14.95	
		489	Doing Business Over the Phone: *Telemarketing for the '90s*	$12.95	$14.95	
		496	Motivation & Goal-Setting: *The Keys to Achieving Success*	$12.95	$14.95	
LIFESTYLE		415	Balancing Career & Family: *Overcoming the Superwoman Syndrome*	$12.95	$14.95	
		416	Real Men Don't Vacuum	$12.95	$14.95	
		464	Self-Esteem: *The Power to Be Your Best*	$12.95	$14.95	
		484	The Stress Management Handbook	$12.95	$14.95	
		486	Parenting: *Ward & June Don't Live Here Anymore*	$12.95	$14.95	
		487	How to Get the Job You Want	$12.95	$14.95	

SALES TAX All purchases subject to state and local sales tax. Questions? Call **1-800-258-7248**	
	Subtotal
	Sales Tax **(Add appropriate state and local tax)**
	Shipping and Handling **($1 one item; 50¢ each additional item)**
	Total

VIP#705-008422-093